Kipper was watching television. He was watching a programme called "The Angry Giant". He liked the programme.

The angry giant lived in a castle near a village. Nobody in the village liked the giant. He was always cross.

When the giant was cross he stamped his feet and the houses shook.

"Oh no!" everyone said. "He's cross again. He's always cross."

Kipper went to find Chip but he was out.
He picked up the magic key and it began
to glow.

"Ooh!" said Kipper.

He ran to get Biff but she was out with
Chip. The magic began to work. It took
Kipper inside the magic house.

The magic took Kipper to the gate of
the giant's castle. Kipper was frightened.

He saw a signpost. It pointed to the village. He didn't want to meet the giant, so he went to the village.

Kipper came to the village but it was
tiny. Kipper was a giant.
"Oh no!" said Kipper.

"Go away," yelled the people. "We don't want you. We've got one giant. We don't want another one."

The people threw things at Kipper.

"Go away," they yelled. "We don't want another giant. We don't want you."

"Stop it," shouted Kipper. "I'm not a giant. I'm a boy."

The people said, "Well, you look like a giant."

Kipper began to cry.

"I'm not a giant," he said. "I'm a little boy and I don't like this adventure."

"Giants don't cry," said the people.
"Perhaps he is a little boy but he looks like
a giant to us. Perhaps he can help us."

Kipper helped the villagers to mend their
houses. He put back the broken roofs.
"Good old Kipper," everyone said.

"The giant threw this big stone at us,"
said the people. "We don't want it here.
Can you put it outside the village?"

"Yes," said Kipper, "I'll try."
He picked up the stone and took it outside
the village.

"Good old Kipper!" everyone called.

All the people liked Kipper.

"Thank you," they said. "You have
helped us a lot."
The village band played for him.

The giant came back.
He was very angry when he saw Kipper in
the village.

"I'm the giant here," he shouted.
He ran towards the village. Crash! He fell
over the stone.

"Ouch!" he yelled.

The people were frightened but Kipper
went to help the giant. He picked up the
giant's things and put a bandage round his
head.

Kipper was bigger than the giant.
"Be a good giant," said Kipper. "Stop
being angry and the people will like you."

So the giant stopped being angry.
"I'll try to be good," he said.
"Hooray!" shouted the people. "Let's
have a party!"

The key began to glow.

"It's time for me to go now," said Kipper. "Goodbye. Thank you for the party."

The magic took Kipper home.

"Nobody likes an angry giant," said Kipper. "What an adventure!"